For Pippa
~ HE

For Lydia, thank you for
believing in me
~ NT

Caterpillar Books
An imprint of the Little Tiger Group
www.littletiger.co.uk
1 Coda Studios, 189 Munster Road, London SW6 6AW
Imported into the EEA by Penguin Random House Ireland,
Morrison Chambers, 32 Nassau Street, Dublin D02 YH68
First published in Great Britain 2022
Text by Harriet Evans
Text copyright © Caterpillar Books Ltd 2022
Illustrations copyright © Nia Tudor 2022
With thanks to Kevin Anderson & Associates
A CIP catalogue record for this book is available from the British Library

ISBN: 978-1-83891-432-5
CPB/2800/2117/0222
10 9 8 7 6 5 4 3 2 1

FSC
www.fsc.org
MIX
Paper from
responsible sources
FSC® C017606

The Forest Stewardship Council® (FSC®) is an international,
non-governmental organisation dedicated to promoting
responsible management of the world's forests. FSC operates a
system of forest certification and product labelling that allows
consumers to identify wood and wood-based products
from well-managed forests and other controlled sources.

For more information about the FSC,
please visit their website at www.fsc.org

WHEN YOU JOINED OUR FAMILY

LiTTLE TiGER

LONDON

Harriet Evans

Nia Tudor

When you joined our family,

I knew you were just who I'd waited and wished for.

When you joined
our family,

I was so excited to
bring you home.

I've been excited
to have you in my life...

...every day since.

When you joined our family,

everything must have seemed new and strange.

We spent time together, and you learned
that I will always keep you safe.

When you joined our family,

I signed papers that promised we would belong to each other forever.

I am proud to
take care of you.

When you joined our family, you met my loved ones...

...and I knew that they would love you too.

When you joined our family,

I realised that whoever was special to you
would be special to me too because of you.

You can always talk about your story with me.

When you joined our family,
I knew that however different
we may look from each other...

...it is the love in our hearts that binds us together.

When you joined our family, I vowed to celebrate the ways you are unique...

...and the ways we are alike.

You are so special to me.

When you joined our family,

I thought of the questions
you might have as you grow.

I might not always have
the answers, but we can
seek them together.

When you joined our family,
I promised to take care of you
in the happy times...

...and also in the sad
and angry times.

I will celebrate you, come what may.

When you joined our family,
we made our own traditions.

I treasure the time we spend together.

When you joined our family,
you made each day worth
the waiting and wishing.